Defendi Antônio da Silva

A HEMOPHILIAC'S MEMOIRS

A TRUE STORY

1st edition
FLORIANÓPOLIS
2024

Título: A HEMOPHILIAC'S MEMOIRS: A TRUE STORY
Copyright © 2024 Defendi Antônio da Silva

Revision
Defendi Antônio da Silva
Typesetting and Editorial Coordination
Fabiano Medeiros Florentino
Cover
Defendi Antônio da Silva

S586m Silva, Defendi Antônio da

A HEMOPHILIAC'S MEMOIRS: A TRUE STORY /
Defendi A. da Silva. – 1ST EDITION – São José - SC. :
Despertando Talentos, 2024.
104 p. il. ; 21 cm.

Inclui Pensamentos; fotos.
ISBN 978-65-5415-040-8

1. Hemophilia - Patients - Biography.
2. Hemophilia - Psychological aspects. 3. Mourning.
I. Silva, Defendi Antônio da. II. Título.

CDD B 869.098164
CDD B 808.882

Gráfica e Editora Despertando Talentos
Rua Paulino Júlio de Souza, 1351 - Ipiranga - CEP 88111-590
São José - SC
Tel .: Cel .: +55 (48) 98440-5411
E-mail: editorasdt@gmail.com
Site: www.graficadespertandotalentos.com.br
Facebook: editoradespertandotalentos

ACKNOWLEDGMENTS:

To all the doctors and health professionals in general, who in my constant walks through hospitals, medical clinics and clinical analysis laboratories, treated me with humanity and dignity. Thank you.

To my father and my mother (already deceased) who raised hemophiliac children in a very difficult time for medical resources. "Anonymous heroes". Thank you very much.

To all my blood brothers, companions on this journey, especially my sister Maria das Dores (Ica-already deceased) who helped me a lot. Thank you.

I OFFER THIS WORK TO MY SWEET WIFE ZILMA, FRIEND, COMPANION AND MY GUARDIAN ANGEL embodied HERE ON EARTH, I OWE HER FOR THE BETTER HUMAN BEING I AM TODAY. THANK YOU.

DefendiAntônio da Silva

INTRODUCTION

In this book, I will recount my experiences as a hemophiliac, from childhood to adulthood. I will try to faithfully describe everything I saw and lived through as a hemophiliac and, above all, as a human being on this long journey of life. In the second part, I will talk about my beloved son Jackson, who passed away before I could finish the book. My wish is that this work conveys to each reader the importance of family, human warmth, and companionship in facing the difficulties of everyday life. A hug to all and much peace.

NOTE: Hemophilia is a hereditary blood clotting disorder that causes bleeding. It is caused by a deficiency in the quantity or quality of clotting factors VIII or IX. There is hemophilia A, with factor VIII deficiency, and hemophilia B, with factor IX deficiency. My family carries the gene for hemophilia A.

INFORMATION: It is estimated that there are about 1,000 hemophiliacs in the state of Santa Catarina, 13,000 in Brazil, and 350,000 in the world. Note: Data researched on Google.

DEFENDI ANTÔNIO DA SILVA

Part 1...09
Part 2...79

7

PART 1

I was born in Urussanga, Santa Catarina, on December 25, 1959, a Friday, but my father only registered my birth on Monday, so my birth certificate shows the date as December 28, 1959. However, my mother always maintained that December 25, 1959, is my real birth date. Many people have told me that I should be called Natalino (meaning "related to Christmas" in Portuguese). Incidentally, I have never met anyone named Natalino. However, Defendi is a fairly common and normal name in Criciúma, as there is a neighborhood there called São Defende. According to my mother, this was the inspiration for my name, but the person who wrote my birth certificate spelled it as it is pronounced, that is, with an "i" at the end. Or was it a brilliant idea of my father's? "Mystery."

Looking at the historical archives, I found that the President of Brazil in the year I was born was Juscelino Kubitschek de Oliveira. Other facts and curiosities of the time include:

* The Brazilian soccer champion was Bahia.

* In music, Celly Campelo was enjoying success with "Estúpido Cupido" (Stupid Cupid).

* Kolynos was the number one toothpaste.

* The headache medicine was Melhoral.

* The film "Ben-Hur" won 11 Oscars, a record only equaled 31 years later by "Titanic."

* Fidel Castro installed the first communist government in Latin America.

* Construction began on the Belém-Brasília highway, with 2,100 km (1,305 miles), under the leadership of engineer Bernardo Sayão, who died during construction when a tree fell on him.

* "Grande Hotel" (Grand Hotel), "Cruzeiro," and "Seleções" (Reader's Digest) were the leading magazines; of the three, only "Seleções" still survives.

* Volkswagen began mass production of the car that would become the best-selling car in Brazil: the Fusca. I had a 1972 Fusca 1500.

DEFENDI ANTÔNIO DA SILVA

My mother had 14 children, namely:

* Maria das Dores (deceased)

* Marta (deceased)

* Mario (deceased)

* Manoel Francisco (deceased)

* Maura

* Maurina

* Maurílio

* João (deceased)

* Donato

* Defendi

* José Tadeu (deceased)

* Gabriela

* Nazareno Salvador (deceased)

* Antônio (deceased)

My mother, Maria de Lourdes Fernandes Madeira da Silva, was always a housewife, a woman of strong temperament. If she said black was red, you had to agree. But at the same time, she had an enviable character. My father, Antônio João da Silva, was a coal miner in the Santana neighborhood in Urussanga, Santa Catarina. He retired early due to respiratory problems. He was a calm, serene man with a natural authority; he only had to look at his children, and they would obey. I never saw him hit a child.

My parents lived well until the 1960s, then came the setbacks, disagreements, and fights, which culminated in their separation in the early 1970s. It was not infidelity, but certainly, in my opinion, the weariness, scars, and wear and tear of a difficult life were the main factors. Imagine raising 14 children in such a difficult time, noting that four died as babies: Marta, Manoel Francisco, José Tadeu, and Nazareno Salvador. Antônio was stillborn.

As stated on the cover, this book is a true story. I will try to transcribe here real facts and events that I remember from the 1970s onward, when I was already 11 years old. I will also rely on accounts from my siblings who are still alive. If my parents were still alive, they would certainly be my faithful source of research and more accurate dates. But since this is unfortunately not possible, I have to try to give a beginning, middle, and end to this story, trying to make the facts make sense and have meaning and, mainly, to engage the readers who may be willing to read the book.

12

DEFENDI ANTÔNIO DA SILVA

From 1970 backward, I have vague memories of significant events in our family. I have some reports from older siblings, such as the certainty that my father and mother never imagined that the health problems their sons faced were related and caused by hemophilia. Even the boys who died as babies certainly had problems caused by hemophilia. Of the nine sons my mother had, only one, Maurílio, is not a hemophiliac. But how do we know if the four who died as babies were hemophiliacs? Logically, from the reports of my mother and older siblings. The problems the children had, today it is known with clarity and certainty that they were caused by hemophilia.

Certainly, at such a distant time when nothing was known about hemophilia, the problems we faced related to this disease must have been many. How difficult and painful it must have been for my mother and father to raise and care for hemophiliac children at a time so far removed from medical resources. In fact, they didn't even know what hemophilia was, as there was no effective treatment at that time. It was a practically unknown disease, even in the medical community. My parents only learned that hemophilia was the health problem of their sons in 1982 with the death of João, then 24 years old. I will detail this fact further on. With confirmation of diagnosis, there are four of us: me, Donato, Mário (deceased), and João (deceased).

13

In the 1970s, despite not knowing we were hemophiliacs, the four of us survivors were already struggling and going about our lives. I can't even imagine how my parents managed to deal with the day-to-day problems that every child certainly has, but a hemophiliac child has many more, and there were four small hemophiliac children. Nowadays, despite all the resources available for the treatment of hemophilia, it is known that a child with hemophilia needs a lot of attention and care. Imagine that in a distant time without resources. I often catch myself thinking how sad my mother must have felt when she saw us with some trauma, especially in the joints, which hurt excessively.

I remember very well an event that happened to my brother João, more or less in the middle or towards the end of the 1960s. At that time, we were already living in Laguna; my parents were taking care of a cattle ranch. At that time, we used to walk barefoot, and one day João cut his foot on a shard of glass. The cut was deep, and the impressive thing is that the blood spurted upward like a jet. I can't describe the accident in detail, but I remember my mother immediately and very worriedly putting coffee powder on the cut and tying it tightly with a cloth.

It was what could be done at the time; my brother wasn't even taken to the hospital. In my

14

DEFENDI ANTÔNIO DA SILVA

opinion, it wouldn't have made much difference, I believe, but certainly, even at such a distant time when nothing was known about hemophilia, coffee powder would not have been the resource adopted in the hospital. We were very humble, and my mother did what she could and knew. The cut took some time to heal, and in the first few days, every time the cloth was removed to clean the area, the blood still spurted upward; it was frightening. Today, I think my brother ran a great risk of getting an infection or tetanus, and even of dying at the time. But fortunately, he got better and was fine.

On that farm, my parents took care of cattle and planted crops. I can't imagine what the deal was between my parents and the owner. My younger siblings and I spent our days playing, typical games of the time, like marbles, spinning tops, hide-and-seek, among many others. I think there was a positive side to not knowing about hemophilia when we were kids. First, because there was no adequate treatment, and second, not knowing the reason for the frequent episodes caused by hemophilia, we automatically led a theoretically "normal" life and played without any worries. However, it is very important to point out that the after-effects that are notorious in hemophiliacs of my time are due to the lack of adequate treatment and the lack of care that is necessary in the daily lives of people with hemophilia.

15

A HEMOPHILIAC'S MEMOIRS: A TRUE STORY

Nowadays, this treatment that improves quality of life exists, as well as information on the necessary care, especially in the case of children. Here in this book of memories, I will adopt my way of telling stories, that is, I will write down the facts, events, and daily life of the family as I remember them. They will be findings from my memory that will certainly be somewhat out of context. Another episode that certainly had to do with hemophilia happened to my brother Donato, I believe in the late 1960s. It was during a move we made from Criciúma to Laguna. For days he had been bleeding from a tooth, and on the day of the trip, he was very weak. In fact, I remember that Donato suffered from frequent bleeding from his teeth.

I have very little memory of that trip, but according to my mother's accounts, there was a mechanical problem with the truck in Tubarão, and they had to stop to call a mechanic. During this waiting time for the truck to be repaired, someone came by selling popsicles. We all got one, including Donato, and to everyone's surprise, as soon as he finished his popsicle, the bleeding from his tooth stopped. My mother always told this story. Unfortunately, she never learned about the great benefit of ice therapy for hemophiliacs and for other purposes. My brothers and I only really learned about the great importance of ice therapy for trauma from the year 2000 onward. It was a

16

shame and lost time, because today it is known that it is a great ally in the treatment of hemophilia. How many traumas and little problems of the past would ice treatment have helped, and a lot.

Currently, I do ice therapy daily after physical activity; I am recovering very well the lost time. We had a complicated childhood and youth due to hemophilia, certainly with several unwanted visits from it. But we were so small and indifferent that we faced the situation with resilience, despite the pain and difficulties caused by the limitations. But time went by, and life went on. Despite the difficulties imposed by hemophilia, we did have our childhood. We ran, played ball, and played many other games. I think that in this aspect (as I have already commented) it was even positive that we did not know that we were hemophiliacs, because nobody kept saying: "Don't do this, don't do that, you might hurt yourself." It was all allowed, but the consequences were accumulating, and the negative balance is something we, the hemophiliacs of the old guard, know and are very familiar with, that is, the irreversible after-effects and limitations.

But in our childhood purity and oblivious to reality, we were happy, yes, even because for us, everything was fine. We didn't have the age or maturity to think about what frequently happened to us. The traumas and problems arising from hemophilia came and went, sometimes with a lot of pain, sometimes not so much. We cried, we complained, but when it got better, it was back to normal life. But certainly for my mother and father, the reality was quite different. They knew that we had a problem that was different from other children, and it was serious, but they didn't know what it was, so I suppose they suffered a lot because of it.

I remember that we used to play a lot of soccer, and we usually had injuries to our ankles. This area hurt a lot, especially at night when it was time to sleep, as it was almost impossible to relax our feet on the mattress. We cried a lot until sleep overcame us. The trauma and consequent pain in the joints of a hemophiliac is intense and responsible for many after-effects of a past without knowledge of the disease and without treatment. My mother always commented that Mário was the one who had the most difficulties with trauma and after-effects in childhood and that because of this, he started walking very late and with many difficulties.

A trauma in any joint of a hemophiliac, besides causing a lot of pain, results in a very long and slow recovery, even with current treatments. This highlights the importance of care and prevention through prophylaxis, which is now offered free of charge by the Ministry of Health to all hemophiliacs.

18

DEFENDI ANTÔNIO DA SILVA

As children, we cried a lot because of joint pain, and my mother's sadness was visible as she couldn't do anything to alleviate our suffering. In truth, she did what was possible in those days, which amounted to tea, and pills like Melhoral Infantil and Cibalena — full of acetylsalicylic acid, which we know today is harmful for hemophiliacs.

Another thing my mother always asked my father to buy was alcohol, which we would apply to the site of the trauma. I don't know to what extent this helped (if it helped at all), but it was another option we had, and I think the placebo effect contributed to its perceived effectiveness, because we used it with faith and conviction that it was a remedy. This is more or less how we lived our childhood and adolescence, according to my memories.

Thankfully, there were also good times in the past, and they were well worth living. I think it's good to acknowledge this because the past is gone, and it's not healthy to dwell only on bad things, giving way to negativity. On the other hand, I have to be aware that I am writing a memoir, so I have to try to report the facts as faithfully as possible. Therefore, I have to bring my accounts closer to the full reality of the past and present, without being dramatic, just the truth.

19

A HEMOPHILIAC'S MEMOIRS: A TRUE STORY

I remember an event that happened with Mario in 1970. We lived at the time on a small farm far from the city. The place was difficult to access, and the interesting thing was that to get to where we lived, you had to pass through another property, with the owner's authorization, of course.

At that time, Mario used to have frequent nosebleeds. It was June, and for days he had a nosebleed to the point of becoming extremely weak. Nothing my parents did worked, and the bleeding wouldn't stop. I don't remember what they did to try to stop the bleeding. It was a time when home remedies were widely used, especially in the countryside, and they did work for many ailments. However, for hemophilia, it logically wouldn't work. Neither my mother nor anyone else knew that it was a spontaneous hemorrhage (without trauma) caused by hemophilia.

I remember my brother very well, always with a cloth to his nose in an attempt to stop the blood. He would soil several cloths throughout the day. The situation became so critical that he was taken to the hospital. Relatives who didn't live in Laguna came to visit him, as they were informed of his serious clinical condition due to several days of continuous bleeding.

I don't know which doctor treated him at the time or what was done, but a few days later he

20

DEFENDI ANTÔNIO DA SILVA

returned home and the bleeding had stopped. But in my humble opinion as a hemophiliac, it must have been more or less like this: as the bleeding came spontaneously, in the hospital, with the help of some medication, perhaps serum, and insistence on feeding, the bleeding also stopped spontaneously. After all, at the time we didn't even know we were hemophiliacs. *However, I remember, despite being young, that my mother said that someone we knew donated blood for a transfusion for my brother. Maybe that's why the bleeding stopped and my brother got better.

The date he was admitted to the hospital is perhaps the only one I will remember in this memoir: June 21, 1970, a Sunday. It was the World Cup final in which Brazil became three-time world champions. Logically, an unforgettable date for anyone who loves football as much as I do.

We lived for a while on this small farm. I don't know exactly how long. It was a very nice place to live at our age. The house was a few meters from the sea, where we played a lot. We spent our days by the sea, sometimes hunting, sometimes fishing, setting traps, taking care of caged birds, etc. Good times, despite the difficulties of everyday life. We were 11 people living in a small wooden house without a bathroom. I honestly don't remember how we used to bathe and relieve ourselves. My parents worked in the fields, and we lived basically from the harvest, some fishing, and my father's small pension.

During the time we lived on this farm, I don't have memories of many problems with hemophilia. Certainly, there were some, but they went unnoticed and were treated as everyday occurrences. Surely, there was pain and sleepless nights. However, I remember one event that was quite impactful and hard to forget. I remember it was a Saturday afternoon. We were in a cart, me, my mother, and my brothers Maurílio, João, and Donato. The destination was the church in the Portinho neighborhood, where Donato and I had classes for our first communion.

I remember that my mother, Maurílio, and João, who was driving the cart, were sitting on the bench. Donato and I sat on the floor facing the bench. The cart, pulled by a mare, was at a considerable speed, and at a certain point my right foot slipped out and hit the wheel at speed. My foot almost went between the bars of the wheel. It all happened so fast that I just let out a little scream that wasn't even noticed by my mother. At home, Maurílio said he noticed the situation, but since I didn't complain, he didn't say anything. But the fact is that the impact was big, and when we arrived at our destination and later at home, my ankle was extremely swollen and hurting a lot. I imagine it was several days of pain

22

DEFENDI ANTÔNIO DA SILVA

and crying, as a trauma to a hemophiliac's joints causes a lot of pain and takes a long time to recover, especially at that time when we didn't know we were hemophiliacs, let alone had any treatment.

...

Finally, in the 1970s, we moved to our own home, a large wooden house built by my father, with the help of Mário and Maurílio. It was a much better place to live, as it was very close to school, church, some shops, and the city center. Today, the wooden house built by my father logically no longer exists, but I still have relatives who live there. At this school, which still exists today and is called Renato Ramos da Silva, I was able to complete my elementary education without many problems that I can recall. The interesting thing is that it was only much later that I understood why my mother, whose authority we respected very much, forbade us from running and playing ball.

I respected her but didn't obey much, and sometimes I came home limping, and then came the scolding. I was even ashamed of my classmates who knew that I didn't participate in the games on my mother's orders, it wasn't always possible to circumvent her vigilance, as the school was very close to our house. But today I understand perfectly that she only wanted to protect me from possible traumas arising from my problem.

23

A HEMOPHILIAC'S MEMOIRS: A TRUE STORY

I did my old gymnasium (current middle school) at CEAL, at that time I was already a teenager and I remember 3 events that occurred during the period I studied at this school that marked my life excessively. The first happened during recess, I was playing soccer (now it was difficult for my mother to watch over me), I took a blow to my left ankle that swelled a lot, I went back to the classroom and when it was time to leave, things got complicated, I could practically not put my foot on the floor. How was I going to walk 30 minutes to my house?

I should have asked for help at school, but I didn't ask out of shame, and I went limping, stumbling, to my house. It was late afternoon, winter, it would soon be night. But it was at that moment that my guardian angel or a benevolent spirit decided to help me, glory to God, one of the school's janitors who also lived in the Portinho neighborhood saw me and asked what had happened, she knew about my problem, we used to call her Dona Bê, she asked me to stay where I was and that she would send a son to pick me up by bicycle (only rich people had cars in those days), and so her son took me home on the back of his bicycle.

I don't remember if I thanked her and her son, I was a teenager and maybe I didn't even realize the good they did for me, certainly without their help I wouldn't have gotten home in that condition. My

24

eternal gratitude to them and may God bless them wherever they are. I don't remember what I told my mother, but I suppose she didn't need to, as she must have imagined the reason. The fact is, I must have missed several days of school, in addition to the pain that a joint trauma causes.

An episode of bleeding in the joints of a hemophiliac takes a long time for complete recovery, even today, even with the resources that are already available, imagine in times so far from resources as that time. Hence the reason why so many hemophiliacs of my time have joint sequelae. Certainly all this was not good for the head of a teenager, it was very difficult to understand why we hurt ourselves so easily and our colleagues didn't, and there was also the aggravating factor that the traumas took days and sometimes months to improve, still running the risk of some permanent sequela depending on the severity of the trauma. In fact, when I was young, I was very ashamed of being this way, and I didn't even know what my problem was, and I knew about my brothers.

Our consolation was our mother's affection and crying until we got better. But life went on. The second event was quite complicated and when I remember it, a movie plays in my head, I was going by bus from school to home, when I pulled the bell for the bus to stop, I was already going down

25

the steps of the door, it happens that the driver in question had the habit that when he was pulling over to the shoulder he was already opening the door and I, with the bus in motion, got off, it was almost stopped, but I missed the step and as I was very skinny I took a spectacular fall, I still remember vividly my body floating in the air and me hitting violently first with the back of my head on the asphalt and then one side of my hip also hit the asphalt hard. Immediately I managed to get up and I put my hand on the back of my head which hurt a lot, I was dazed and perplexed by what happened in a matter of seconds, only the conductor got off and asked if I was okay, to which I said yes, he then got back on the bus and they continued on their journey.

If it were today, it would result in an omission of help on the part of the driver and the conductor and consequently a lawsuit against the transport company, but those were distant times and we were also very humble, I think we didn't even know that there were lawyers and justice to plead for rights. I arrived home crying and in pain and my very worried mother wanted to know what had happened, I remember that nobody went to the company mainly to question this driver who was known for this habit of opening the bus door before stopping, I also understand that I had my share of the blame, because I should have waited

26

DEFENDI ANTÔNIO DA SILVA

for it to stop completely, before getting off. I was left with a huge bump (hematoma) on my head and difficulty walking for a long time, and to think that I wasn't even taken to the hospital. I was sick and limping for a long time, although it was, as far as I remember, the end of the school year and I, a good student that I was, had already passed the year, thank goodness, otherwise I would run the risk of losing the year because of the accident.

The Bible in Ecclesiastes 3.2, says: there is a time to be born and a time to die. So on that day, with God's blessings, my guardian angel was on duty and supported me in the air, because what came after was profit in the face of the serious fall I had and being a hemophiliac, and the most impressive thing is that I wasn't even taken to the hospital and there were no after-effects from the accident, really for those who believe, as I believe, it was a blessing from God. I don't remember what the days after the accident were like, but they were certainly very difficult and painful. The side of my hip that hit the asphalt I remember that I was limping for a long time because of the accident, but the hematoma on my head I don't remember if it took a long time to improve. I do remember headaches. But time passed and I got better.

The third event that resulted in a huge setback both physically and psychologically, was the result of a prank with a schoolmate, a silly prank that should never be played by anyone, especially a hemophiliac, we were playing a game of giving a penny on the thigh, for those who don't know, it was actually a foolishness that consisted of kneeing someone who was distracted in the thigh. That day I had given a penny to a colleague and time passed and I even forgot about it, but he didn't forget and at a time when I was completely oblivious to what had happened, and it was in this moment of oblivion that he gave me such a well-placed one that my leg went numb and I felt right away that the prank had gone wrong for me, and it did go wrong.

It was the end of November and consequently the end of the school year for those who hadn't been held back, and I passed straight through and wouldn't be retaking it, so I would be on vacation the next day. It was difficult to go home, as my thigh was already quite swollen and this time no one showed up to help, how I got home I can't imagine, but it must have been very difficult, painful and time consuming. The result of childishness was the entire holiday limping and in daily pain, unable to play, which caused me great sadness. Logically I wouldn't do such a stupid thing if I knew I was a hemophiliac. I don't remember what I told my mother, but I certainly hid the truth, otherwise the scolding would come.

DEFENDI ANTÔNIO DA SILVA

I still remember that the following year, when classes started, I was still having trouble walking. I honestly don't remember if I took any medication, and even if I did, it would have been the pain relievers of the time, nothing else was done because we didn't have anything else and we didn't even know we were hemophiliacs. Time and God healed me and life went on. Thus we arrived in the 80s, I was 20 years old and started working, from that time onwards I remember several events, both in my life and in the lives of my family members, and if I remember in detail and don't forget any, wow, there are a lot of stories to tell.

If they were still alive, my parents would certainly have many stories for me to tell and report in this book, imagine how many episodes related to hemophilia they must have experienced at the time when we were babies, then growing children and that we didn't know, and that will not be reported here because these probably difficult episodes, both for us, the 4 hemophiliac children, and for my parents, must have been very difficult, and it certainly was. Imagine raising 4 children with hemophilia in such a distant time and without medical resources and specific medications, in fact, we didn't even know that the so-called hemophilia existed. From the knowledge of a layman and reader of the subject, hemophilia is a disease with very old reports, but with very recent medical and medicinal

29

resources. How many families in the world have had the same problems we went through, including consequent deaths.

Hemophilia at a time when it was not known and consequently had no medication was considered a very serious disease, because there is a risk of spontaneous internal bleeding. Trauma to the joints and muscles takes days or even months to recover, even with current resources. Today, there are treatments that improve the quality of life of hemophiliacs, but care and vigilance in avoiding trauma that causes bleeding episodes must be constant, speaking of bleeding, in hemophiliacs everything is more difficult. For those of you who are reading this book and are not familiar with hemophilia, I will briefly explain what happens in the event of bleeding in a hemophiliac with factor VIII deficiency.

We all have clotting factors, which are blood proteins, they are responsible for healing when bleeding occurs, we have several clotting factors. Now imagine that I have bleeding from a cut on my arm, the clotting factors will spring into action like a relay race, that is, factor I hands the baton to factor II, and so on until it reaches the site of the bleeding and together with the platelets heal the cut, but in my case there is a problem in this race there, that is, when factor VII goes to hand the baton to factor

30

DEFENDI ANTÔNIO DA SILVA

VIII, in my case it is weak, because it is deficient and the race continues slowly, which can aggravate the bleeding.

But thank God, today we have intravenous factor VIII, which helps a lot in the treatment of hemophilia. When we still didn't have the diagnosis of hemophilia, a disease totally unknown to us, I remember my mother saying that we had rheumatism in the blood, I can't say how she arrived at this diagnosis, whether by herself, someone's suggestion or by some doctor. So for me and my other hemophiliac siblings, we suffered from rheumatism in the blood, and I even said so at school in order to be excused from physical education class.

How naive, because it was precisely for this reason that I stayed in my first job for a very short time. One day, I don't remember why, I told my boss that I had rheumatism in my blood, the next day he called me into the office, told me some things that I don't remember and fired me, but he didn't mention that the reason was the supposed illness, but I was sure that this was the reason, it was a small market and I didn't even have a formal contract. Today, this market no longer exists. What an irony of fate, huh?

I lost my job because of a disease I didn't have, and if I had known the real disease I had, I would certainly have been fired too. But fortunately things have changed in that regard, these days everyone can work, whether or not they have health problems, but continuing with the 1980s, life went on normally between the inevitable episodes of trauma and bleeding, but still without knowing the main cause. My brother Mário retired very early due to disability, he was always very sick and had many sequelae in his joints, he also used to bleed a lot from his nose. Donato and I worked at that time in a factory of cement artifacts and construction materials, it was a very heavy job and we had many difficulties.

The tile manufacturing service was very heavy and the beginner always started there, it was routine and common for people to start in the morning and not return in the afternoon. Imagine how difficult it was for us hemophiliacs, and it was very difficult indeed. Donato started at the company before me, but he didn't stay long, at that time, due to health problems, my mother frequently took him to the hospital in Laguna with health problems, he managed to work for a very short time and soon also retired due to disability.

I remember that my adaptation to the service was not easy, I thought about giving up on the same day, but I was very ashamed, as I had already given up on a similar service at another company, then

32

DEFENDI ANTÔNIO DA SILVA

my wounded pride spoke louder and I managed to overcome and adapt to the service, but it was really tough, I would arrive home with sore and calloused hands even wearing gloves. Thank God I didn't have any problems related to hemophilia in the first few months, so little by little I was overcoming and adapting to work.

It was really hard work, especially for me, who at that time was very thin, which is why I was even discharged from military service. But in this service there were also some strong employees who worked normally and even laughed at those who gave up and called them lazy. I worked for a year and three months at this company and many days due to trauma resulting from hemophilia I missed work, I got a medical certificate or went to work sick facing difficulties that only God and I knew how difficult it was, physically and psychologically it was very sad the situation.

Once, a company driver, seeing my low income, called me lazy, I have no hard feelings, because just as I didn't know the reason for my limitations, he didn't know either. Some time later, the company started to have financial problems, had to reduce the number of employees and I was fired. And so we arrived in the year 1982, which began calmly and culminated in very sad events and the discovery of hemophilia.

It all started with the sudden illness of my brother João (now deceased), he had been working at Angeloni as a butcher for 5 years, he was tall and had a very good physique and appeared to be in good health, he was 23 years old and one day he arrived home from work early saying he had a stomachache and the pain intensified and at night he was taken to the hospital in a very worrying situation for the family, I believe he had been feeling this pain for days and didn't report anything, because very quickly his clinical condition worsened and only got worse, he spent a week in the hospital in Laguna without any improvement, given the worsening situation, the manager of Angeloni at the time advised the family to request a transfer to a hospital in Criciúma, and so he was transferred to Hospital São José.

The exams showed that he had a strangulated ulcer in his stomach, that's what they used to say, today they say perforated, I think both terms are correct, given the very serious condition he had to have emergency surgery, without anyone knowing that my brother was a hemophiliac. That's when the problems worsened and my brother's fight for his life lasted for over 40 days. It was a period of much suffering and pain for him mainly and for the whole family.

34

DEFENDI ANTÔNIO DA SILVA

After the surgery, it seemed like he had improved, but it was short-lived. He started having serious bleeding problems, which made his doctors suspicious. Through specific tests, they discovered he was hemophilic. They must have asked my mother something about the family that led them to suspect and request the exam that confirmed the diagnosis. I remember those days were filled with anguish and suffering for him and our family who witnessed it all.

My mother was never the same. She stayed by his side until his very last day. He was a tall, strong man, but he lost weight and withered away day by day. It was extremely sad to see, and it left a mark on all of us. The doctors did what they could and started treating him with cryoprecipitate, the medication used in those days to treat hemophilia, in addition to blood transfusions. The cryoprecipitate was produced in Florianópolis, but I think that due to the severity of his condition, there wasn't enough medication. If it were today, we would have concentrated factor VIII, a modern and very efficient medication, but even so, we know that to perform a major surgery like the one my brother had, he would have to be very well prepared, and even then, there would be the inherent risks of any surgery.

Nowadays, you hardly hear about ulcers. Healthcare is more advanced, and people can

35

diagnose gastritis through tests and treat it with modern medications. Unfortunately, my brother wasn't so lucky; otherwise, he wouldn't have even had the surgery. He suffered a lot. His weight loss was shocking, and many relatives didn't want to visit him anymore. After more than 40 days of suffering, my brother unfortunately passed away.

After his death, our family life changed radically. My mother, as I already mentioned, was never the same person. She suffered too much from all those events she witnessed from beginning to end, even though she had hope for his recovery until the very end. At the funeral, she cried, saying she never expected this to happen to him, as he had been healthy until then. Days after his passing, the diagnosis of hemophilia also came for me, Donato, and Mário through tests. Maurílio escaped; he won the lottery. Of all the sons, he is the only one who is not a hemophiliac. The following months were very difficult. My sister Maura fell into a deep sadness that lasted for months. She went to the cemetery almost every day and stayed there for hours, sometimes under a scorching sun, which may be the reason why she later developed skin cancer.

But time, that great ally of life that helps us overcome the turbulences and stumbles life throws at us, passed, and little by little, each of us resumed our lives. My mother never went to the cemetery

DEFENDI ANTÔNIO DA SILVA

again after my brother's death, not even on the day of the burial. Her life was reduced to collecting her pension and doing her daily shopping at the market. At that time, my parents were already separated, and since, in those days, separation was almost always synonymous with being enemies, he did not attend the funeral. Time passed quickly, and in July 1982, I went to live in Cocal do Sul with my older sister Maria, whom we all called Ica. At the time, I was unemployed and went to try for a job at Cerâmica Eliane, which was already a very strong and modern company at the time. I managed to get a job at this company, but it's a long and complicated story in my life.

The Eliane Group was already a very organized company and a very good place to work, as it offered good salaries and several benefits to its workers, but to join the company, you had to go through some stages and criteria, starting with an individual aptitude test, where many candidates were already eliminated. If approved in this test, the candidate was referred to any available general helper vacancy in any sector of the company.

But before that, you had to go through the company's medical and dental services. I was approved in the test and referred to a vacancy in the company's Refractory sector, but there were still consultations with the company's doctor and dentist. The medical exam went smoothly, as I was young and, until then, did not present or appear to have any health problems. Still, I was advised by my sister and my brother-in-law, who already worked at the company, not to mention that I was hemophilic. Otherwise, I would hardly be able to work there.

Things got complicated at the dentist's. A dentist named Luiza saw me. I sat in the chair, and she observed that my teeth were in good condition. However, there was a tooth in the back of my lower left jaw that had to be extracted. When I saw her preparing to extract it, I quickly got up from the chair and said that I would come back another day, but I didn't say it was because of the hemophilia, as I was afraid of not being accepted into the company if I told them, and that would certainly be the case.

The dentist found my attitude very strange and understood that it was fear. I remember her telling me that without extracting the tooth, I wouldn't be able to work at the company. Imagine my disappointment and sadness. The fear of losing the opportunity in a large and modern company was enormous. That's when I started to understand that hemophilia was beginning to impose limits on me. But neither I nor my sister gave up on finding a solution. We put the company on hold and went looking for a dentist at the SUS (Brazilian public health system) in Criciúma, a city very close to

38

DEFENDI ANTÔNIO DA SILVA

Cocal do Sul. It is worth remembering that Cocal do Sul was not yet a municipality and was part of Urussanga, my hometown. We went to Criciúma because it was a more prosperous city with more medical resources.

Well, at the SUS clinic, we talked and told my story to a dentist named Dauro, who treated me very well. He agreed to extract the tooth, but I would have to be hospitalized to carry out the procedure. This dentist was part of the medical staff at Hospital São José, and he himself arranged for my admission. Then he spoke with the Director of the Blood Bank (at the time, there was no blood center), Dr. Everaldo Sabatini, about the need for a blood transfusion. This doctor already knew our history with hemophilia, and so it was agreed that I would have the tooth extracted in the Surgical Center.

The tooth was extracted, and I still remember the dentist telling the assistant that the bleeding was normal. I had been admitted the day before, and on the third day, in the morning, I had a fever. Since there had been no bleeding until then, I don't remember what procedures and medications were done before and after the extraction, but I can say that nothing that would be done today was done then. Nowadays, hemophiliacs can undergo any dental procedure as long as they take the necessary precautions and care, which are now possible.

39

A HEMOPHILIAC'S MEMOIRS: A TRUE STORY

After being discharged, I went back to my sister's house. Everything seemed fine, and there was no bleeding. However, at nightfall, I suddenly felt that gush of blood, and there began my ordeal and also that of my sister, who was always by my side. The tooth was bleeding a lot, enough to frighten anyone, especially my sister, who certainly remembered the recent death of my brother. We took the bus and went to Hospital São José. When we got there, the dentist who had performed the extraction was called, took me to the dental surgery room, sutured the area, and sent me home, saying that everything would be fine.

But it wasn't. Until then, I don't remember ever feeling so much pain in my life, and the bleeding wouldn't stop. In the morning, we went back to the hospital, and I was admitted.

It's unbelievable, but because of that tooth, I spent 30 days hospitalized, and the bleeding wouldn't stop. My sister was desperate because it had been less than six months since my brother João had passed away, and my mother didn't even know about my situation. I had many blood transfusions, saline solution, and cryoprecipitate, and nothing worked. The site was even cauterized with silver nitrate. I don't even know what silver nitrate is, but I remember very well the doctor who performed the procedure at Dr. Everaldo's request.

But that didn't work either. The concern of everyone involved was visible, even because they knew about my brother's case. But I, perhaps because I was young and unaware of the gravity of the situation, was calm and never really thought the worst, even when Dr. Everaldo told me that they were doing everything possible and that they had even looked for cryoprecipitate in Curitiba.

I also rinsed my mouth with ice water many times, but to no avail. They were already thinking of transferring me to a hospital in Florianópolis when Dr. Dauro, who had extracted the tooth, made one last attempt that ended up working. He had the idea of making a dressing with denture adhesive. I was taken to the dentist's room, and there, after cleaning the area well, he made the dressing that thankfully solved the problem.

I could barely close my mouth or chew properly, so I spent over 15 days eating soft, almost liquid foods. Thankfully, the bleeding stopped, and a few days later, I was discharged to go home, still with the bandage. Everyone was relieved, especially my sister, who had been very nervous about the negative events and certainly blamed herself for advising me to have the tooth extracted. But everything turned out well, thank God. 20 days later, I went to Dr. Dauro's office, and he removed the bandage. I was very apprehensive and nervous that day, but

41

fortunately, after removing the bandage, the dentist said the area was completely healed.

Those were difficult and apprehensive days for everyone, but I am very grateful to my sister Ica, who helped me a lot. Even with three small children, she didn't miss a single day at the hospital. I can imagine how difficult it was for her, first because of my difficult situation, and then she had the housework, her husband who worked, the children to take care of. My sister deserves all the applause. When we are young, we don't even realize these situations, we live almost oblivious to these important and necessary details. How difficult it must have been for her for over 30 days to go back and forth from Cocal do Sul to Criciúma, how many household chores she had to leave behind to worry about me, and the fear that the worst would happen. How would she tell my mother?

I don't remember thanking her and my brother-in-law Valdir for everything they did for me. Out of inexperience, and not out of malice, I never thanked them. Here, in these simple memories, I thank them very much and ask for forgiveness. Today, thank God, I recognize that I was wrong, and I try to always be a better and fairer human being. My sister, unfortunately, is already on the other side of life. I wish her much light and the blessings of the Divine Master Jesus.

DEFENDI ANTÔNIO DA SILVA

With the tooth problem solved, I returned to the company's dental office, and coincidentally, it was the same dentist who saw me (the company also had a dentist). I don't recall how the conversation with her went, if she said or asked me anything. I think that because of the time that had passed without seeing me, she even forgot about me. With the tooth extracted and the others in good condition, she cleared me for work. I returned to the recruitment and selection department, where the well-known boss, called Carlão, was surprised that I wasn't working yet. However, I didn't tell him everything that had happened.

A few days later, I was referred to a vacancy at the refractory factory in the foundry sector, and so, again, perhaps by irony of fate, another difficult stage in my life due to hemophilia began.

The work was very heavy. It's difficult to explain here, but the sector where I went to work required a lot of strength in the arms and legs, and I was very thin. I didn't have the strength necessary to perform the service. I never understood why they didn't choose stronger people for the sector. But I insisted, and after 15 days of work, I had an injury (bleeding) in the back of my right thigh that prevented me from working. So, I was sent to the company's medical department. I had no choice but to tell the doctor that I was a hemophiliac.

43

A HEMOPHILIAC'S MEMOIRS: A TRUE STORY

He didn't like the fact that I had omitted it and treated me very badly. Today, I even think I was wrong, but on the other hand, there was the doubt whether I would be given a job opportunity. It was very difficult for me, still so young, to deal with a situation that was difficult to solve and even controversial, due to the total lack of knowledge about hemophilia by people and even doctors who were not hematologists (specialists in the area). I really wanted to work because I needed to help my mother. And the doctor practically kicked me out of his office and didn't give me a medical certificate. I don't remember how many days I was out of work, but it must have been 20 days or more.

My thigh hurt a lot. I couldn't stand up because the pain was intense and getting worse. A huge hematoma developed in the entire back of my thigh. They were again days of uncertainty and fear of losing my job, which, in my mind, was almost certain. But I was young and had a good capacity for recovery, and I didn't give up. I got better and went back to the company. Now the whole factory knew about my case. I went to talk to the general manager. I don't remember what we talked about, but the conversation was short, not least because he was already aware of the situation, and he sent me to the division head. It was he who would decide my fate.

44

DEFENDI ANTÔNIO DA SILVA

The division head was called Clédio Fachin. He asked me a series of questions and inquiries about hemophilia, which I don't remember. All I know is that they were totally out of context questions. He even asked me if hemophilia was contagious. In fact, it was an unknown disease to him. At one point in the conversation, he got up from his chair and said he was going to talk to the general manager and told me to wait in the room. Some time later, he came back and said they were going to give me another chance, now in the refractory box classification sector, which were used for tile burning, a much lighter job.

I was sure I would be fired, but to my surprise, I wasn't. It was said in the company that because it was an election year, they weren't firing anyone because the son of the patriarch/owner and founder of the company was a candidate for State Deputy. I worked in this sector for a long time without any problems. Later, when I was already quite settled in the company, I got a position in quality control through the good friendship I had with the head of that department and, of course, also through my own competence. And so I continued with the ambition to grow professionally, as there was this prospect for being a large company with the potential for it. Thus, through an internal competition, I got a position in the office in the planning department.

45

Those were times of calm and professional fulfillment, as I reached a good stage in the company and with a good salary, and the best thing about all this is that I started to help my mother much more, who really needed it, and at that time, I was helping to raise 3 grandchildren. I never imagined, not even for a moment, that after so many setbacks I would get where I did in the company and with only a high school education at the time. But unfortunately, hemophilia would visit me from time to time and continued to cause me problems and limitations and caused me to visit the company's medical service. In the 8 years that I worked there, I went to the medical department countless times, and always for the same reason, that is: hemophilia. I was hospitalized several times at the São José Hospital in Criciúma.

I remember one day I was working, it must have been around 9:00 in the morning, and my nose started to bleed. I went to the sector's infirmary, and they put cotton in my nose, but the blood wouldn't stop. So, with my boss's authorization, I went to the company's doctor. I was already a regular customer there and well known by the people in the sector. Even the doctor who had treated me badly some time ago changed his attitude towards me.

Now the doctor knew my history and also knew that there was nothing he could do there, and

46

DEFENDI ANTÔNIO DA SILVA

he referred me to the Criciúma hospital. The social worker accompanied me and stayed there until the hospitalization was carried out. I remember that my nose bled for over 24 hours without stopping for a moment, and it only stopped after the administration by infusion of cryoprecipitate, the medicine used at the time. I don't remember how many days I was hospitalized, but it was only a few days.

To this day, I don't know who told my sister Ica that I had been hospitalized because I didn't live with her anymore, but rather in the company's accommodation, which was very good. She must have told me, and I forgot. Days later, I was already 100% recovered, I went back to work, and life went on normally again. Cerâmica Eliane was a great company to work for, and a fair one. I had many health problems there because of hemophilia, and I was never fired, and I also always had the support of my superiors. When I left the company, it was because I resigned, a fact that today I admit was negligence and also lack of experience on my part. So much so that some time later I regretted it.

In 1984, I had a very serious problem that resulted in a 30-day hospitalization at the University Hospital of Florianópolis, 15 of which were spent in the ICU. Regrettably, it was again a consequence of a playful act. It's impossible to be aware and conscious 24 hours a day that you have a health problem and need to be careful, especially since no one imagines or foresees a setback, whatever it may be. As I mentioned, I was young at the time and tried to live my life normally and without worries. Logically, today I think differently and try to take care of myself as much as possible.

This is how the accident happened: After dinner, which was served in the company cafeteria, some colleagues who lived there and I were walking back to the dormitory, joking along the way. At one point, I pretended to kick a colleague in the head. I was wearing flip-flops with smooth soles, and when I lifted my left foot with a certain speed, the supporting foot that was on the asphalt slipped. I took a tremendous fall, hitting the bone on the right side of my hip hard on the asphalt. I got up quickly, but I already realized that there would be a problem. When I got to the dorm, the area was already quite swollen, and a huge bruise quickly formed at the site of the impact, and the pain was very intense. Late at night and in a lot of pain, I asked the dorm guard to call the company's on-call staff to take me to the hospital emergency room, but the problem was that at night they could only take me to the hospital in Urussanga. The on-call person left me in the emergency room and returned to Cocal do Sul.

The emergency room doctor saw me, prescribed some pain medication that I don't even remember, and told me that he could admit me until the next day, but that they didn't have the resources to treat my case and that I should go to Criciúma. I decided not to be hospitalized there and asked the receptionist to call the on-call staff and returned to the dorm, still in a lot of pain and walking with great difficulty. I was alone, without any family, just me and God, an extremely difficult and even desperate situation.

It was a night of great pain and without any medication. I couldn't sleep a wink. The next morning, with great difficulty, I took the bus and went to the São José Hospital in Criciúma. I waited a long time in the emergency room until I was seen. The doctor who saw me admitted me and said that the hematologist who already knew me would see me and medicate me, but unfortunately, he could only stop by the room in the early afternoon. When he saw me in that situation, crying in pain and with the area very swollen, he had no doubts and told me that he would transfer me to Florianópolis, because in Criciúma there would not be enough cryoprecipitate to treat the severity of the bleeding that was evident and increasing rapidly. It is worth noting, for those who are unaware of hemophilia, that when a person with normal levels of factor VIII, that is, who is not a hemophiliac, suffers a significant trauma as I did, that person will also certainly have problems, but will not go through the difficulties that a hemophiliac goes through.

A HEMOPHILIAC'S MEMOIRS: A TRUE STORY

At the end of the afternoon of the same day, I was transferred to Florianópolis, accompanied by my sister Maura, who lived in Laguna and was visiting our sister Ica's house. It was an extremely difficult and uncomfortable trip, as the ambulance was a Chevrolet Veraneio without the slightest stability. It is also worth remembering that at that time the roads were terrible. The ambulance shook a lot on the uneven road, causing the bed to sway a lot. This increased the pain and the severity of the bleeding at the trauma site. What a day, trip, and unforgettable and cruel night! Only God in heaven to give us strength to overcome the trials of life. It was hours on the road and when we got there, the driver began the pilgrimage to find a hospital that would accept me, because I wasn't sent to a specific hospital. I don't remember how many hospitals the driver went to until he was able to get me admitted. I can't say if the reason for the refusal was lack of beds or conditions to treat a hemophiliac in the condition I was in.

Finally, after driving around a lot, the university hospital agreed to admit me. I was in a very critical situation due to the terrible trip. Now it wasn't just the trauma site that was swollen, but the bleeding had taken over my entire leg to the point that my knee had disappeared. The pain was unbearable, and the doctor on duty sedated me. Imagine the situation: I was going on two nights

50

in pain, sleepless, and without any medication. I don't know how many hours I slept. The next day I went up to the room. The pain continued without a second's relief, only sedation. I lifted the sheet to take a look at my leg and was terrified by the size of the swelling. It looked like I had no knee, terrifying. My leg turned a yellowish color. All this was the result of the terrible trip, the lack of therapeutic resources at the time. Today it is known that for a hemophiliac who suffers a trauma as I did, the first step is rest to avoid worsening the situation and immediately start the treatment available today.

The pain was so intense that I couldn't fully relax my body in bed. The impression I had was that only my head and heels were touching the mattress. Uncontrollable crying was the only way not to go into total despair. I still clearly remember two nurses in the room looking at me moved and very sorry for me and the doctor saying that she was going to transfer me to the ICU. Again, there were many turbulent days. I was sedated several times a day. It was the only way to relax and get some sleep. I even asked to be sedated, such was the pain I was feeling.

I was very well attended at the H.U. hospital, both by the doctors and the nurses. The overall care was already excellent at that time. I am very grateful for the H.U. hospital, even today, as I still go to the

A HEMOPHILIAC'S MEMOIRS: A TRUE STORY

H.U. for treatment and follow-up of hepatitis C, and the treatment continues to be good. The treatment with cryoprecipitate and other medications began to take effect, and a few days later I was thankfully pain-free, although my leg was still very swollen and I had great difficulty getting around.

I spent 15 days in the ICU. There, despite the intensive treatment, it was very difficult because of the conditions I was in, totally in the hands of doctors and nurses. It was 15 days of lying on my back, unable to turn or move my body. My parents, and especially my mother, suffered a lot with my situation. After this critical period, I improved and was moved back to the room and began treatment with ice on the trauma site. I think I spent more than 40 days hospitalized on the fourth floor. It seemed like time had stopped for me, such was the longing for family, friends, work, and the world outside. I was already able to go to the bathroom alone with difficulty, and one day, through the transom, I was able to take a look at life outside and saw some people walking, cars, and the blue sky. It was a sunny day. Of course, there was a window in my room, but the view was just another wall of another block of the hospital.

A long time has passed, but I will never forget the humane way I was treated and respected by everyone there. I will also never forget something

52

that I believe I will never experience again today: someone responsible for the food came to my room to ask me what I liked to eat, if I had any preferences. Until then, no one in my life had ever asked me that. And how good and qualified the food was there. I can't forget to express my gratitude to my sister Maura, who interrupted her vacation to accompany me to Florianópolis. I don't remember how many days she stayed in the capital, but it must have been only a few, as she would soon have to return to work. Thank you very much to her.

I also thank my brother Maurílio, who helped me a lot. When the ambulance arrived at the H.U. emergency room, he was already there. Some relative had already warned him, certainly my sister Ica. He must have been looking for me in the hospital emergency rooms and asking for information. Imagine the difficulty at a time when there were no cell phones, and landlines were a privilege for a few. But during the time I was hospitalized, he helped me a lot, including looking for and getting blood donors for me, as there was a need for donors to produce the cryoprecipitate, which was the drug available for the treatment of hemophilia.

Thank you very much to him for his support and concern. I also make a reference to my sister-in-law Rose, my wife's sister and also Maurílio's wife. She went to visit me almost every day, if my memory

53

serves me correctly. She was very young, but already with a very supportive heart. Thank you very much to her for the affection, so important and necessary at a very difficult time. At that time, Maurílio was still single and dating his current wife, Cida, who coincidentally is the sister of my wife Zilma. Later, life united us all through marriage and also friendship. Since the episode of the accident that caused all this upheaval and setbacks in my life and that of my family, it has been more than two months. I imagine how everyone's routine must have changed. There was the issue of distance, work, and daily chores. My mother couldn't even go to Florianópolis to see me. She must have suffered and cried a lot.

When I was discharged, I still had a lot of difficulty walking, but I could go home. Maurílio and Cida accompanied me to Cocal do Sul. It took some time to regain normal movement in my leg, but I had to go back to work, and again that fear of being fired came back. Imagine being fired at a time when I needed it so much and was psychologically shattered. But fortunately, the company understood the situation. I was not fired and went back to work.

Finally, I was healthy again and back to work as usual. If I were to detail everything this accident caused me and the people involved, I think I would run out of paper, such a large book it would be. But it's enough to mention the essentials without

54

DEFENDI ANTÔNIO DA SILVA

dramatizing, because it's in the past and we all have problems in life to overcome with faith. And so the difficult days were left behind, and new challenges would certainly come. After this event, I had a good break from hemophilia and lived without worries.

That's exactly what the life of a hemophiliac is like, full of ups and downs, challenges, and uncertainties, especially when there was no effective treatment. We are war veterans, accustomed to living with difficulties.

My life and work routine at the company continued normally without major problems until, in 1987, I faced another serious issue. I learned something I never imagined could happen: hemophiliacs could also suffer spontaneous bleeding. Until then, I thought it only happened when I suffered some trauma or accident, but that wasn't quite right.

One day, out of nowhere, I started to feel discomfort on the right side of my spleen. At first, I didn't care because I was very healthy. However, I started to have pain and difficulty moving. By now, I was more educated and attentive to my health, so I sought out a hematologist at the São José Hospital in Criciúma. She examined me and immediately ordered an ultrasound, which revealed internal bleeding in my spleen. The doctor admitted me, and that same day, I was in the ICU.

A HEMOPHILIAC'S MEMOIRS: A TRUE STORY

I spent 15 days in the ICU, but thank God the bleeding was restricted to the spleen area without major consequences. With absolute rest and cryoprecipitate, I recovered well. I had no pain, but the area remained very sensitive for a long time.

I went back to work, but some time later, I returned to the hematologist for routine exams and monitoring of the lesion (hematoma) through imaging. The ultrasound always showed that the lesion was there, but after a year or more, it disappeared, and my spleen was left without any sequelae.

In 1990, I resigned from my job to work for myself. It was a wrong and disastrous attitude that I later regretted. I had a history of overcoming challenges at Grupo Eliane, and I threw it all away out of sheer immaturity and inexperience. I lacked reflection and ignored the advice of people who opposed my decision.

My mother and my sister, Ica, repeatedly advised me not to quit, but I was relentless, fixated on the idea of working as a freelancer. I hadn't even prepared for it – a typical move of a young and empty-headed person who didn't think about the consequences that could arise from such a reckless decision. Unfortunately, when you are young, you have the false illusion that you are the owner of the truth, and you ignore the voices of experience that

DEFENDI ANTÔNIO DA SILVA

try to warn you. Then, when life hits you in the face and you wake up to reality, it may be too late. That's exactly what happened to me.

I left a stable job at a large company where I had worked for eight years, had many friends, and earned everyone's respect for my history of overcoming difficulties. And for what? To set up a small bar in a trailer, in a rented spot, in a field I had no knowledge of.

But life teaches us that nothing is by chance, and everything has a reason. Nothing happens to us that is not meant to teach and mature us. Some people don't learn, but I learned a lot. However, I still need to learn much more because life keeps tripping us up, and many times, we contribute to it.

I was immature, inexperienced, a stone to be polished. But thank God, I was never a bad person, nor did it ever cross my mind to do any harm to anyone. I have always had a lot of faith in God, and that always gave me the strength to get back on my feet and follow my life's script, which, as we all know, is full of crossroads and mysteries.

I have had many challenges in my life, and I know I will have many more. But I thank God for all the opportunities I had to become a better person through difficult times. It is precisely in those hours that one learns the greatest and best lessons. You just have to pay attention and reflect because we are here in this world of trials and tribulations to evolve and learn to be good.

I ran the bar for ten years, and after a lot of work, struggles, and learning, I was able to make a living from it. But in the beginning, it was a huge challenge with many moments of uncertainty. 1990 was also the year I married my wife, Zilma. We have lived together and in love to this day, and I believe forever, if God in his infinite mercy allows it. In addition to being my beloved companion, she is my great friend and confidante, and she helped me run the bar and overcome challenges.

Some relatives also helped me with the bar work. I won't mention everyone's names, but thank you all for everything. And I apologize for being a pain. I was way too demanding, but today I am very different. Life teaches, and people learn when they want to.

Regarding hemophilia, I was living a quiet and calm moment. But it wasn't long before I was once again the negative protagonist of a new problem — that is, directly responsible for what happened.

A wooden house belonging to my sister, Maurina, had been demolished, and another was built in its place. The wood from the old house was piled up right next to where I needed to place the

DEFENDI ANTÔNIO DA SILVA

ladder to carry out a service on the new house. I put the ladder on top of the wood and climbed. When I was on the last step, preparing to carry out the service, the ladder slid on the wood and slipped. I fell along with the ladder and took a very hard blow to my right shin, which hit the step of the ladder. It was a terrifying situation. I felt a sharp pain, and when I looked, I saw a huge hematoma forming on my shin.

The sadness and frustration at having committed such recklessness were enormous. But young hemophiliacs are like that. When we are well, it's normal life, and we forget about certain precautions and ignore the negative eventualities that can occur due to our negligence. Besides, let's face it, no one can take care of themselves all the time, no matter what age. But the truth is that I was very irresponsible with myself, and it cannot and should not be like that.

This accident caused me a lot of problems. I tried to go to work at the bar, but I felt a lot of pain in the area, and the hematoma was huge. The problem was that now I lived in Laguna, far from any medical resources for hemophilia. I ended up not even going to the doctor, and so I continued to be neglectful of my own health.

I don't remember what kind of medication I used at home, but as time went by, a wound formed in the area, and the hematoma hardened. I started to get worried and went to the SUS pharmacy. The nurse cleaned the area and removed all the clotted blood. When she finished cleaning, the sight was impressive. My shin, which is very thin, was left with a huge hole from the injury. In the first dressings, a significant amount of gauze was placed over the wound.

I spent over a month getting dressings changed every day. I came to think that it would never heal. But over time, the dressings became smaller, and the area healed, although the scar is still there today.

After that accident on the ladder, I don't remember any other serious ones, only the routine episodes that I was already used to dealing with. They were milder episodes, and as there was no adequate medication, the solution was to rest and wait for time to pass. Trauma to the joints, in addition to causing a lot of pain, is the main reason why many hemophiliacs from the past live with irreversible sequelae. I myself have several, and I don't even remember how they happened.

Until about 1992, both of my knees were preserved. It was around that time that I had a spontaneous bleed in my left knee, which swelled a lot and left a sequela that greatly limits my knee movement. Currently, with a diagnosis of osteoarthritis, my knee is quite compromised, and I am facing a possible knee replacement.

60

DEFENDI ANTÔNIO DA SILVA

If this knee problem had happened at a time when I already had the resources that are available today, I certainly could have had a different story. I remember that the day before I felt something strange in the back of my knee, like a tingling sensation, it was already the bleeding starting, but I ignored it and the next day I traveled to Florianópolis by bus, and there my knee swelled up a lot. I was visiting my father-in-law, I should have gone to the doctor, but I didn't because I had to work. I returned home on a very difficult trip, with the negative balance of a time when there was already some treatment for hemophilia, but I lacked the responsibility and discipline with my health that today, thank God, I have in abundance. I could have avoided a series of disorders and limitations that this knee has caused me over the years. If an episode like this happened today, I would know exactly how to act without even needing to go to the doctor at first, because we already have the medicine at home and we are well oriented by competent medical teams at HEMOSC, where we have a very efficient and humane treatment and follow-up.

2001 was the year that began another very difficult phase in my life, it was when I discovered through a phone call from HEMOSC (Criciúma) that my serology was positive for hepatitis C. The facts that I will describe here about the impact that the discovery that I had hepatitis C had on me, may even be considered by some as bizarre, but it is a true fact that really happened. Currently it is known that there is a cure in almost 100% of cases for hepatitis C, but unfortunately until the year 2000 I had never heard of hepatitis C, until one Sunday I was watching the program Domingão do Faustão and the country duo Sandro and Gustavo were singing, who were very successful with the song "A Garagem da Vizinha", but the main subject of the program was the duo's stoppage for 6 months because Sandro had hepatitis C and needed to be treated, but the fact is, that at that time the singer Sandro died and the idea that I had about the case, and by total ignorance, was that hepatitis C killed in 6 months after diagnosis.

The incident with the singer had happened some time ago and I didn't even remember it anymore, then when I received the phone call informing me of the diagnosis and advising me to see a doctor to get treated, my head immediately went haywire and I automatically remembered the singer's story and I already saw death in front of me, look what a horror, and all because of a little lack of knowledge. I was 41 years old and my only son was 7 years old, and the fixed thought was that I was going to die too in 6 months, my world fell apart, only bad and negative thoughts came to my head, a situation of true nightmare and dread.

62

DEFENDI ANTÔNIO DA SILVA

I looked for a general practitioner, reported the case and he started to give me accurate information and to reassure me, also asked me to do some specific tests to analyze my situation regarding the liver, because it is known that the hepatitis C virus attacks the liver's defense cells. But I, in my ignorance about the subject, wanted to know everything and asked the doctor hundreds of questions, but the doctor said what was necessary, because each case is different and differs from patient to patient.

I started to try to understand the disease, but unfortunately at the time I did not have the resources of the internet, the information was given by doctors and some literature that I bought, and as I informed myself by reading and asking, the worse I got psychologically, I became an obsessive, annoying and negative person and only thought and wanted to talk about it, perhaps a supposed depression that I ignored. When I discovered that the disease can be asymptomatic for many years without giving any signs, I got even more worried, because I imagined that I had had the virus for many years and that I would have little chance of a cure, I suffered in anticipation.

Everything I felt was related to the disease, it was impressive, a real neurosis, how fragile we are and how much we need God and family in these

63

hours. And it was precisely by God and the support of the wonderful family I have that I didn't succumb, that I didn't go crazy. I have always been a man of great faith since I was a child, a reader of the Bible since I was very young and I never lie down or get up without first saying my prayers, and I have been doing this for many years in good times, and also in bad times. And it was in faith and in the support of my family that I was able to gradually overcome the turbulence.

I thank God very much for the wife I have, because she was my safe harbor who understood me and helped me a lot in this delicate moment of my life. During the year 2002 I followed up with a general practitioner, but I was not satisfied, there were many doubts that generated questions and few answers, I could not understand why I was having altered specific test results and was not prescribed any medication, although I was clinically well or apparently, I don't know what the correct expression would be. It was then that I discovered that the doctor who treats hepatitis C is the gastroenterologist.

I made an appointment with Dr. Jorge Tadeu Zanini (now deceased) and from that appointment things took a new turn, because besides being a very competent doctor, he explained to me in detail what I still didn't know and hadn't heard, and reassured me

64

by saying that there were already good medications to treat hepatitis C. However, this doctor did me a great favor and referred me to be treated with Dr. Esther Dantas, a reference according to him in the treatment of hepatitis in the state.

In March 2003 was my first appointment with her, in her private practice, a truly spectacular doctor who gave me a new reference in my life so full of doubts and uncertainties. After the appointment she referred me to be treated at HEMOSC in Florianópolis, because she worked there at the time and it was all through SUS.

I am a perfectionist, I like things right and well explained, and I was distressed because I did not understand the peculiarities of the treatment of hepatitis C, but Dr. Esther Dantas masterfully explained everything to me right and in detail, and so gradually and over time I came to understand and get used to living with hepatitis C. But it was difficult to know to be a carrier of a serious disease that still did not have a standard and effective treatment. I started 2004 preparing to start my first treatment (there were 3), my transaminases were very high and Dr. Esther decided to start the treatment that would be for one year, it was a treatment with ribavirin + pegylated interferon, I was informed that the side effects would be quite significant and they were.

A HEMOPHILIAC'S MEMOIRS: A TRUE STORY

I followed the doctor's recommendations to the letter, I took good care of myself and ate well, but even so I lost a lot of weight. Ribavirin did not cause me side effects, but according to the doctor it lowers the hematocrit a lot, and it did. The interferon was one injection per week, this one had terrible side effects, both physical, clinical and psychological. I remember the first application of interferon, it was in the morning, I even thought that I would not feel many effects, because I spent the whole morning well, but in the early afternoon I began to feel little by little some chills that were intensifying to the point that I was shaking all over my body at a very intense rhythm that even scared me, immediately my wife gave me a dose of Tylenol drops, and little by little the fever and chills were diminishing.

It was a very bad and scary feeling, because I never imagined that the effects would be like that, something I had never felt in my life. In the following doses I didn't have the chills anymore, but the indisposition due to this treatment, in my case was daily, I had a lot of muscle pain in the lumbar region that bothered me too much, I also had constant fever, and to think that I used this medication for a year, only God in heaven and my family know how difficult a year it was for me. I always had a lot of faith and despite the difficulties I never stopped praying and believing in the cure.

66

DEFENDI ANTÔNIO DA SILVA

But the first treatment shook my emotional structure, to the point that I even had suicidal thoughts, I even thought about stopping the treatment, I lost a lot of weight, I was pale, but thank God I managed to take the treatment to the end. In the sixth month of treatment I did the specific test for hepatitis C and it was negative, the treatment was responding, according to the doctor if it was positive I would have to stop the treatment, because it would not be worth continuing, and I continued until the end of the year, another thing that worried me a lot was the fluctuation of my platelets, which because of the interferon dropped a lot to the point of fluctuating between 50,000 to 25,000, a situation that worried Dr. Esther a lot and me mainly. So it was determined by the doctor that I should only do interferon if the platelets were at least 50,000.

I used to have my platelet count checked weekly, and waiting for the result was always a worrisome and distressing experience. The treatment ended in early 2005, and some time later, 30 days if I remember correctly, the doctor ordered the specific test. To my sadness, the result came back positive. According to Dr. Esther, there had been a relapse, meaning that after stopping the treatment, the virus became active again. In fact, today I can say with certainty that, given Dr. Esther's experience and competence, she already knew this could happen, as my transaminase levels were never within the normal range during treatment.

Despite the frustration, life had to go on, and I continued to feel psychologically down. However, there was a force inside me that told me to move forward and have faith, and faith was something I never lacked, as I never stopped praying, not even for a single day. The doctor talked to me a lot about the importance of continuing follow-up with routine exams, taking good care of myself, especially with my diet, and waiting for a new treatment with other medications that should arrive soon.

And taking care of myself was what I did most after being diagnosed with hepatitis C. I started to have a disciplined life in every way. I can say with certainty that this discipline helped me a lot to arrive in 2012 in good shape for a new treatment. But in the meantime, before the 2012 treatment, other events happened, some positive, others negative. In May 2005, my brother Mario passed away at the age of 56, a victim of laryngeal cancer. He was a heavy smoker and suffered greatly from this disease. He had to undergo a tracheostomy and went through many difficulties during treatment. Those were very sad and difficult times for both him and the whole family. May he rest in peace.

From 2003 onwards, I started treating hemophilia at HEMOSC (Hematology and

DEFENDI ANTÔNIO DA SILVA

Hemotherapy Center) in Florianópolis, and from then on, a lot changed in my life regarding hemophilia. I started to receive treatment and guidance from competent doctors in the field of hematology. I learned to better understand the disease and realized that hemophilia treatment protocols had changed and improved significantly, and I didn't even know it.

I learned that I probably contracted the hepatitis C virus in one of the many blood transfusions I had. Factor VIII, the medication for treating hemophilia, was already a reality and available to have at home and use in case of need. I also got to know the Hemophilia Association, a place where hemophiliacs who do not live in Florianópolis can stay while undergoing some type of treatment. It is a place with excellent support structure for hemophiliacs, with meals and humane treatment from the staff working there.

I attended the Hemophilia Association between 2005 and 2006, going there three times a week for physiotherapy. It was a very good period because there I met many people with problems similar to or even more complicated than mine. I also started to see hemophilia differently with the help of the professionals working there. In other words: hemophilia is a reality that we have to face and take care of, but there we are helped to improve our

69

self-esteem and not victimize ourselves. The motto is: positive thinking and life goes on responsibly.

At a time when I was emotionally wrecked, getting to know and attending the association was very good for me. In 2007, two hematomas appeared on my right thigh. One disappeared over time, but the other brought me problems. I noticed that it was increasing in volume and I had to stop physiotherapy because, in this case, it would only aggravate the situation if I continued to strain the area. I sought out Dr. Denise at HEMOSC and she requested some exams. Based on her evaluation, it was concluded that it was a pseudo-tumor.

Dr. Goulart, who at the time was the orthopedic doctor at HEMOSC, drained it (removed the blood volume) twice, but as time went by it would fill up again and increase in size, causing a lot of discomfort. I started to have limitations in walking, and that worried me. It was then that it was concluded that the solution was to remove the hematoma surgically. I was on the SUS (Brazilian Public Health System) waiting list for three years, a very difficult, worrying, and distressing situation. I also noticed Dr. Denise's concern, but she couldn't do anything given the slowness and bureaucracy of the SUS waiting list.

Fortunately, in 2014 I managed to get the money to pay for the surgery, which was performed

70

DEFENDI ANTÔNIO DA SILVA

in a private hospital. I am very grateful to Dr. Denise and Dr. Goulart, who helped me a lot and got me the surgery at a price I could afford. The surgery was performed by Dr. Goulart, a doctor of unquestionable competence (those who know him know). And the surgery was a success and everything went well, thank God. The day after surgery, in the room, Dr. Goulart commented that he thought it would be a small incision, but it wasn't what happened. Due to the many successive hemorrhages at the site, there was a lot of dead tissue throughout the thigh, so he had to make a larger incision to remove and clean it well. There were 33 stitches.

The postoperative period was very smooth and without pain, and also without bleeding. Some time later, with some exercises, I was fully recovered and well, leaving only the scar, memories of difficult years of waiting and overcoming, and also of much faith. Just to report: when the SUS called me to have the surgery, it had been more than three years since I had the surgery. In total, it was more than six years of waiting in line, but I don't complain, everything is fine, the SUS has done a lot and has done a lot for me.

In September 2012, I started my second treatment for hepatitis C. It was a combination treatment with three drugs: pegylated interferon, ribavirin, and boceprevir. Again, I had the same reactions to pegylated interferon, but now I also had the side effects of boceprevir, which was a difficult drug to take. It had to be ingested with some type of fat. I used to take it once a day in the afternoon, before that I would eat bread with crackling, or with sausage, it had to have fat, I don't even remember why anymore, but that's not relevant, it's in the past. The time to take this medicine became almost a torture. It was different from interferon, which over time the side effects would subside. This one, on the contrary, was increasing. I even thought I wouldn't make it, but fortunately, or unfortunately, in the twelfth week the doctor told me to stop the treatment because there was no response.

The viral load test came back positive, so it would be unnecessary to continue treatment according to the doctor. And so another unsuccessful treatment came to an end, but I never lost hope of a cure. Besides my faith, which gave me strength to believe, something told me that one day the cure would come. I started to get tougher and more experienced, I researched a lot about hepatitis C, and I was now much better psychologically. After all, more than 10 years had passed since the diagnosis and I was able to understand that in my case the beast was not that ugly.

I have been passionate about reading since I was a child. I think it's a gift I was born with, because

DEFENDI ANTÔNIO DA SILVA

I remember when I didn't even know how to read yet, I used to leaf through magazines of the time and ask an older brother to read to me, and I would be delighted. When I learned to read, I plunged into the wonderful world of comics, Walt Disney, Maurício de Sousa, and so many other authors, and I never stopped. It's been over 50 years of reading, and good reading that has given me a lot of instruction and has helped me express myself and write correctly. I've been reading the Holy Bible every day for almost 30 years now, and I have my own way of understanding the scriptures, without, of course, disrespecting the understanding of others. I have also read over 80 books on spirituality, which focus on the teachings of Spiritism. The study of spirituality has helped me to be a better person, to understand life and God's designs.

Studying the Spiritist Doctrine, I learned that being a Spiritist is not about being religious, it's about being Christian. It's not about displaying a belief, it's about living a sincere faith. It's not about having a special religion; it's about holding a serious responsibility. It's not about surpassing others; it's about surpassing oneself. It's not about building temples of stone, it's about transforming the heart into an eternal temple. Charity is the "essence" of the Spiritist Doctrine.

But let's get back to talking about hepatitis C. From 2013 until the beginning of 2016, I was only doing follow-up appointments every 6 months with exams, but I was clinically very well. I continued taking good care of myself, having a disciplined life without any bad vices, and eating well and correctly.

In April 2016, I started the third treatment, which this time was thankfully successful. It was a combination of 2 medications, daclatasvir and sofosbuvir, one tablet each, once a day. Fortunately, I have no complaints about this treatment and I didn't experience any side effects either. It was an extremely effective and very smooth treatment. In the first month of treatment, my transaminase levels returned to normal. This treatment lasted only 6 months, but after 90 days I had the viral load test and it was undetectable, meaning negative. It was a moment of much joy and happiness, after more than 14 years of struggle and anticipation, the long-awaited day had arrived. They were very difficult and distressing years, only God in heaven knows the difficulties I went through and overcame with much faith, hope and the essential help of my family, without whom I would not have had the strength and psychological structure.

After 6 months, I had the viral load test again and it was negative again, confirming the success of the treatment. Today, after more than 7 years, I have

74

DEFENDI ANTÔNIO DA SILVA

follow-up appointments every 6 months to detect any problems that may arise in a timely manner due to the damage that the virus leaves in the liver. The main cause of hepatitis C infection is through contact with contaminated blood, especially in the past when there was not the care and control that exists today in blood banks, which are responsible for the collection and distribution of blood and its derivatives.

Due to many blood transfusions and blood products that I received in the past, this must certainly be the reason why I was infected. Currently, there is modern and effective treatment for hemophilia that reduces the risk of contamination through blood and blood products to almost zero.

As described in the introduction, I will only relate the memories of my experience as a hemophiliac, but nothing about my personal life and that of my family. Many things have been forgotten, others I couldn't detail clearly, but in my understanding, a memoir is like that, you try to be as faithful as possible, without dramatizing and without inventing, just the truth, although many things may not be possible to remember, but it was what I was able to deliver to the dear readers.

As I mentioned at the beginning of the book, my family will always carry the hemophilia A gene. So, after a long time without any reported cases, in 2015 my niece Eveline, daughter of my sister Gabriela, had a hemophiliac boy, who is now 8 years old. The boy's name is Nathan and he is very healthy and without sequelae, he is also very well cared for by his parents and grandparents. I remember that my niece was even worried about this issue of hemophilia in the family, she even talked to me. I also remember that a factor VIII dosage test was requested at the blood bank and it was normal, from then on the subject was not mentioned again and she got pregnant. As far as I remember, she had a problem-free pregnancy, but during and after labor she and the baby had problems. From what Eveline told me, Nathan had complications arising from Meconium Aspiration Syndrome, which she said led to a generalized infection and the baby was taken to the semi-intensive care unit, but with medication given in a timely manner, the baby improved after days of fighting for his life. Eveline, who had problems with high blood pressure, also recovered well.

During a shift in the semi-intensive care unit, a hematologist saw the history of hemophilia in the family on Eveline's medical record and ordered a blood test on the baby for investigation. Days later, when mother and baby were already at home and in good health, the hospital called and asked them to go there to talk. It was then that they were told that Nathan was a hemophiliac. Nathan's parents went

DEFENDI ANTÔNIO DA SILVA

through many difficult and uncertain moments, because one thing is hemophilia, another thing is to be the protagonist, that is: being a hemophiliac and being parents of a hemophiliac. They were very young and didn't know anything about how to deal with a hemophiliac child, and this was at a privileged time, but it is impossible that millions of uncertainties, doubts and questions do not arise, and you want to solve everything quickly, when it is time that solves everything, and that is exactly what happened, 8 years later Nathan is well and healthy, he does prophylaxis 3 times a week and doesn't even cry anymore, his father is the one who applies factor VIII to him, and life goes on peacefully.

His mother, Eveline, often says that he is a warrior, he went through many difficulties at birth, but today he is a healthy and happy boy. I don't know if there is any test to know if a woman with a history of hemophilia in the family is a carrier (perhaps a hematologist who might read the book could tell us), but this is no longer important, nor relevant, Nathan had to be born and he was born, and he chose Eveline and Petherson to be his parents and form a happy family.

And so I'm finishing the first part of this book, many things have been forgotten, others have not been said because I understand that there was no need. Currently, I am waiting for a prosthesis in my left knee (maybe by the time I publish the book I will have already done it), but very confident and secure about the safety and resources that exist today in the medical field. No one is 100% prepared for the inclemencies of life, but I can say with all certainty that today I am a human being much more prepared for the falls that life throws our way. Thank God the advances in the treatment of hemophilia have been spectacular, so much so that there is already talk of a cure for hemophilia in the not too distant future.

Let's wait and see. I end by saying that hemophilia is still a serious disease. Do you have to lead a normal life? You have to lead a normal life! But you also have to take care of yourself, a lot. I will leave my contact at the end of the book, if anyone wants to communicate or make any comments, I will be available. Hugs.

Part 2

Here I speak of my son, Jackson, who passed away in a motorcycle accident on September 13th, 2022.

This book was initially intended to be a brief account of my life as a hemophiliac. This second part wasn't planned, but unfortunately, during the writing process, my beloved son, Jackson da Silva, passed away. He even got to read the book's synopsis, so it would be impossible to finish this work without mentioning my beloved son.

The world of reading and books is my only vocation and gift. Reading and writing make me feel in my element. So here, at this moment, I can talk about my beloved son without crying. It's impossible to speak about him in detail with anyone without crying. I summarize him like this: a good, obedient, intelligent, studious, honest, and hardworking son. Anyone who knew him and spent time with him knows I'm telling the truth. I can say

79

this because we lived together for 28 years, a total of over 10,220 days and 245,280 hours. He always lived with us, even after he got married.

It's been almost two years, and Zilma and I still live in a state of bewilderment over what happened. We live as if anesthetized to endure the days that have become difficult and bitter. Every day we receive a dose of anesthesia that contains comfort, faith, and hope, given by Our Lord Jesus Christ, the beloved Master. We made the right choice when we decided not to revolt because it would be the total bankruptcy of our faith and trust in God and eternal life.

Our beloved son never gave us a serious problem that caused us anguish. There were some setbacks, but everyone has and will have them. We taught our son to be good, and kindness was already part of his spirit's essence. We all have and will have moments of emotional instability. After all, we are human beings with flaws and qualities like any other. He always listened silently when I reprimanded him, never answering back, even if he disagreed. Only twice, after he got married, as I recall, did he answer me back. But both times, the next day, he apologized. He always saw me as an example of conduct and character, my companion in Criciúma games. While single, he was always with me or his mother at the gym or on other errands.

DEFENDI ANTÔNIO DA SILVA

He liked to do charity work, and the greatest virtue he had, even though he was very young, in college and working, was being a father to Ketynha. The Spiritist Doctrine says that it is a very noble attitude to be a father to other people's children. Logically, the merit is also Kety's, as they, being such a young couple and with other commitments, had the virtue of caring for and raising Ketynha as their daughter. He had (and has) an immense love for Ketynha, which was reciprocated. She was (and is) in love with her daddy, a love from other lives. He himself said that, and I believe it completely. Only God and we who experienced it can understand such love and affection. When he got home, all she wanted was her daddy. Kety herself recognizes this. There were times when he was called to the gym to calm her crying. He would arrive, pick her up, and she would calm down. Sandra, Kety's mother, would even comment: "My God, what love is this." We cry every time we think about these situations, but at the same time, I am impressed by how spirituality and God are unfathomable. Despite not having the adult understanding of everything that happened, Ketynha assimilated her father's passing. We realize that she misses Jackson, but differently. She looks at the photos and says: "This is my daddy."

The other day, we drove past the Flexion gym, and she said, "My daddy's gym." Another day, we were at a snack bar, and she looked at a young man who was leaving and told Zilma that he looked like my daddy. So that's it; the child also has their particular suffering. The memories are many and make us cry, but we cry as much as necessary because the journey is long, and we need to walk. We cannot give up because that would be losing faith in God. My son was (and still is) my happiness, and I never had any problem talking about his qualities. It was always a joy to praise his intelligence and his effort to succeed through work, study, and honesty.

From a very young age, I told him there are three ways to succeed in life with dignity: by working, studying, and being honest. And thank God, my son was hardworking, studious, and honest. I wasn't the best father in the world, and nobody is because the best father in the world is God who gave us "eternal" life. I was a good father and very present in his life, at home, at school, and in everyday life. My son became a scholar in his field. There was a time when he worked at a gas station during the day and went to Unisul at night for college in Physical Education, and this went on for a long time. In 2019, he graduated with a Bachelor's degree in Physical Education. In the same year, he completed a postgraduate degree in Bodybuilding and was studying Nutrition at Uniasselvi, which he would have completed in 2023.

DEFENDI ANTÔNIO DA SILVA

My son became an excellent professional in his field. Those who were his students, and there were many, know the competence he had. He had it because he prepared himself to reach the level he did. He also dreamed of going to medical school later. Jackson was self-taught in Nutrition but decided to go to college to avoid any inconvenience. He was persecuted a lot because of this. I don't know if it was out of envy or because some people seem to be born into this world only to disrupt the lives of "others," but it's okay. If, by chance, someone who tried to harm him reads this book, don't worry, just stop trying to put out the light of your fellow man.

Life has become dull. My son's physical and daily presence is sorely missed. I never imagined I would experience such a situation. We suffer immensely from his absence and longing, but we cannot lose faith and trust in God, who is just and merciful. Zilma and I joined a WhatsApp group in Brasilia. This group is mainly composed of bereaved mothers who have lost their children or loved ones. They are generally tragic losses, due to accidents, suicides, murders, etc. - tragedies that leave scars, pain, and longing that hurt the soul.

There is a lot of fraternal feeling and understanding of each other's pain. This interaction helps us to reflect that, in the face of loss, we cannot be selfish, as countless people have gone through, are going through, and will go through this painful moment. I am very grateful to God for having met this group. Sometimes we see people on social media giving speeches about the loss of a child by a mother, but this person has not experienced such a loss. This is opportunism for the sake of attention. How can you talk about something you don't know? Only a mother knows what it's like, especially when the loss is preceded by a tragedy.

Even today, unfortunately, people cling to old patterns of facing and seeing grief. That is, if the person becomes discouraged with life, falls into bed, etc., someone will tell them: "You can't stay like this, you're going to get sick," etc. But if you react and get back to life quickly, this same person will say: "So-and-so didn't even feel the death of their child." The truth is that these are bad people. People think they are good people, but they live monitoring the lives of others and don't realize that their own lives are adrift.

My advice is this: when you visit someone who is grieving, forget the "everything happens for a reason," or "how are you?" Just give them a hug. Also, avoid comparisons. For example, saying "so-and-so lost two children in an accident" doesn't comfort the bereaved. Every experience, every story, every pain is different. The longing will be the same, but the context is different. The person

84

isn't being selfish and knows that tragedies happen every day.

Someone might say: "Defendi says things that nobody else does." But that's my goal, without intending any offense, because there are already plenty of people talking about the "same old things." I thank God for allowing me to know the Spiritist Doctrine. It's where I found the strength to endure and understand such a difficult trial. I doubt that the Defendi of the past would have been able to move forward with clarity. Spiritism has a spiritual, scientific, and philosophical framework. There's a logical explanation for everything, always in the light of reason and never emotion. But you have to study a lot, and I mean a lot. I've studied a lot, but it's still not enough. That's why I don't consider myself a "Spiritist" yet. To be considered a "Spiritist," we have to free ourselves from all pride and selfishness, the causes of humanity's moral bankruptcy, and acquire humility, simplicity, and charity in the broadest sense of the word. And I'm still a long way from that.

Maybe someone reading this book will say: "Is Defendi always this cold?" Of course not. I'm also a human being, and therefore vulnerable too. I have my limits, but I'm convinced that grieving isn't about self-flagellation and abandoning yourself to show others that you're suffering. That's a total misconception. God doesn't want or ask for that, and neither does the person who has gone to the other side of life. It's hard, it's really hard, but time never goes back, and people have other reasons to live. We have to have faith in God, faith in eternal life, and try to follow life's path, always trying to do our best. But what about people?

Let them think what they want. What matters is knowing that God is the one who sees into our hearts, and that's enough. They say happiness exists, and it does, but sometimes it's colorful, and sometimes it's black and white. Today, my happiness is in black and white, but I'm sure it will be colorful again, and it will be when I have a colorful dream with my beloved son, a sublime encounter of spirits, where I will know with clarity how he is, or through a comforting letter (psychographed) from a trusted medium, or even the reunion in the spiritual homeland.

You know, my son, I learned through studying that there are families who, due to lack of affection and affinity, destroy themselves and fail in this world through hatred, disagreements, bad habits, etc., and then follow the evolutionary process on the higher plane in different scales and paths. But you, your mother, and I, my son, are and always will be united by the bonds of love, affection, caring, and dialogue. We have connections and affinities

86

DEFENDI ANTÔNIO DA SILVA

from other lives. We had our turbulences, yes, but they were necessary for the advancement of our spirits. And I'm sure, my son, that Divine mercy will reunite us again here or in the Spiritual Homeland. Let us never lose faith and trust in God, for "a day is like a thousand years to the Lord, and a thousand years are like a day" (2 Pedro 3:8).

You Know, My Son...

An only child in the heart of a mother and father never seems to grow up. They are always a baby, the reference point and center of attention. I remember you in your mother's belly, coming from the maternity ward, your first steps, the exaggerated care, as we were first-time parents. Doubts and challenges arise, and we fumble and learn. As far as I can remember, my son, we never lost a night's sleep because of you. You rarely cried at night, even when you weren't feeling well. You were always (and still are) a blessing in our lives.

You were a grown-up child, and we still played a little. I was already retired by then, your mother had to work, and I took care of you. I had the privilege, my son, of being a present father, very present. We played ball, spinning top, marbles, dolls, cars, etc. You didn't like to lose, so I told you that in life you win some and you lose some, but you were a child and didn't want to know. But my obligation as a father was to educate you from an early age.

But you were good at everything, my son, and you almost always beat me. I remember your first days at daycare, the anguish your mother and I felt leaving you alone for the first time. Time flew by, and you were already in elementary school, at Renato Ramos, where you studied until high school. You were always a good student and participated in school events: dances, championships, scavenger hunts, etc. But I, as you well know, my son, monitored your performance. That is, you would come home from school and ask if you could go play. I would ask if you had homework, and you would say yes, but you would do it later. And I would say: "Negative, homework first, then you can play." And you would usually say: "But I don't know how to do today's homework." And I would say: "I'll help you, let's go." And so we would put all the materials on the table, and the homework was done regularly every day.

And time went by, my son, very quickly. Your elementary school diploma, your high school diploma, then a break from your studies to start working. We opened JS Diversões, which we ran for almost five years. During that time, you worked for a short time at Librelato, then at the gas station. Some time later, I asked you to leave the gas station, and

DEFENDI ANTÔNIO DA SILVA

we bought a Fiorino pickup truck and started selling soft drinks, and you accepted. You worked hard and never complained. We stopped selling soft drinks, and you started college for Physical Education. It was 2015, the year you married Kety. You had a civil ceremony, so she is your legitimate wife. From the day she came to live with us, your mother and I adopted her as a daughter, because she deserved it. She never gave us any problems, she comes from a good family. And now, my son, more than ever, she and Ketinha are more than a daughter and granddaughter to us. They are the reason we continue on life's journey, and our comfort.

In 2019, you finally graduated with a bachelor's degree in Physical Education, the same year as the accident in Imbituba with the Gol. You were on your way to Balneário Camboriú for your postgraduate course when the car was totaled, but you escaped practically unscathed. It wasn't your day yet, my son. In fact, you had other minor accidents after that, until the one that culminated in your departure, my son, leaving us with so much longing and perplexity that accompanies us day and night. You know, my son, the days will never be the same without your presence. They have become somber. Such absence, my son. I still haven't been able to delete your contact from my cell phone. Sometimes I even think about calling, but you won't be able to answer. You now live on the other side of life, and as Chico Xavier used to say, the phone only rings from there to here. We have to wait the necessary time, but this communication will come one day, we are sure of it. Our faith and trust in God give us this certainty.

Trips, Saturdays, and Sundays will never be the same without you, my son. That Saturday pizza you loved will never taste the same. Remember, my son, you and I had different preferences. I like light, thinner crust, and you liked it thicker. But we always came to an agreement. The days have still been very difficult, my son. It still feels like yesterday that it all happened. Time seems to have stood still. For people, it will soon be two years, but for us, not even a day. But we have faith in God and in life, and we are absolutely certain that you live on in the spiritual homeland and that one day we will meet again.

People don't forget your habits, quirks, and tastes, my son. That's called feelings kept in the heart forever. You know, my son, you had a light (you still do) that bothered certain people, but only those who live in the shadows. But we ignore them, as they must already carry a heavy weight on their backs. May God bless them. What matters is that the people who loved and admired you were many, many. Even the pets at home liked you more than us. Cristal loved to sit on your lap while you were

90

DEFENDI ANTÔNIO DA SILVA

working on the computer. Rex, I was the one who took care of him and gave him his medicine, but he liked you more. The cockatiel, when you arrived home, would sing with joy. I took very good care of her, but a few days after you left, she died.

Oh, my son, how much longing hurts and is a daily companion, 24 hours a day. We sleep and wake up thinking of you. The void that remains is enormous, but you are eternally etched in our minds, hearts, and spirits. When I remember the bond between you and Ketynha, something I can't explain runs through my body, soul, and mind, a feeling of absence and longing that almost, very nearly, makes our psychological structures crumble. When you arrived home on your motorcycle and made that sound with the engine, she would jump for joy and happiness. There are so many memories, my son, that if I put them all here, the book would be too long.

Ketynha, my child, has been going to the Spiritist Center with us. She loves to stay in the center's school while your mother and I attend the Friday night lecture. Afterward, she participates in the healing session with us. The other day, we were coming home from the Spiritist Center, and she looked up at the sky from inside the car and said: "Jesus is up there in the sky, and that other little star is my daddy."

A HEMOPHILIAC'S MEMOIRS: A TRUE STORY

How can one not cry in such a situation? And no one ever said that crying is forbidden. In fact, Our Lord Jesus Christ wept when he learned of the death of his friend Lazarus, and he also anguished as the time of his torture and crucifixion approached. So, we can cry, yes, but out of longing and never out of revolt or self-pity, thinking that we need to show people that we are suffering. There is no need for that. If you have faith and trust in God, that is enough, because only He knows our hearts and our feelings. Whether we revolt or not, time never goes back. Life goes on here, but it also continues on the other side of life. There is countless evidence in the literature, just study and research. And the loved one who has departed does not want us to suffer because they are alive on the celestial plane, and their time for trials and atonement here on Earth is over, but for those of us who are still here, it is not.

The Bible says that there is a time to be born and a time to die. So, if it is determined by God that I will live 90 years, whether I revolt, torture myself, or not, I will have to fulfill the determined time. Happy is the one who makes good use of time to evolve and improve spiritually. Thus, when returning to the spiritual homeland, they will have the benefits of the good they have practiced by merit.

And speaking of spirituality, my son, I have to talk about religion. It's amazing how there are still people who are blind to spirituality due to a lack

92

DEFENDI ANTÔNIO DA SILVA

of study and think that religiosity is everything. It is not! It's impressive how there are still people who kneel to pray and stand up to humiliate those who do not share the same religion. God and Jesus Christ never said, nor will they ever say, that we need to have a religion to save us. You can have a religion, but it should not be a reason for division but rather have the purpose of adding, of uniting, and not dividing human beings. Our obligation is to build bridges that unite human beings and not walls that separate, to understand that there is only one God of supreme intelligence and that He is the same for all religions. What matters to God is our conduct and effort for our inner reformation.

There are good people in all religions, just as there are also bad people. Being of this or that religion will not give you a passport to salvation. That is a fact. The other day, I heard the medium Maira Rocha from Brasília speak a great truth. She said: "Religion is a table where everyone sits and orders a different dish, but everyone eats together."

I am talking about this subject to get to Jackson, who, after getting married, became closer to Umbanda and enjoyed practicing his religion. Zilma and I were never against it because we knew from an early age that he had sensitivity and also because we understood a little about spirituality, even though Zilma really likes the Catholic religion. I have been studying and have become closer to

93

the Spiritist Doctrine for some years now, but this has never been a problem for us, and we always talked about it. But it happens that Jackson was very hurt by some childhood friends who were very attached to him, and when they learned that he was an Umbanda practitioner, they stopped talking to him. Look at how much prejudice, intolerance, and cultural ignorance there is - that is, condemning something without knowing anything about it.

These people do not know that even Jesus Christ did not do this when he was here. In fact, he did precisely the opposite. But it's okay; it's not revolt, just a vent. These people don't need to worry because, after all, we are all brothers. We all have the right to worship God as we please, as long as our conduct is for love and goodness towards our neighbor. "Do you not know that you are God's temple and that God's Spirit dwells in your midst?" 1 Corinthians 3:16.

You see, our body is a sanctuary where the eternal spirit that God gave us dwells. Therefore, we can worship God in church, in a monastery, in a temple, in a Spiritist center, in an Umbanda terreiro, in a public square, etc., because what matters to God is our conduct and the intentions of our hearts. You know, my son, since your departure to the spiritual homeland, I haven't been to the Criciúma stadium anymore. I still can't, my son. You know how much I love soccer, and especially watching it

94

DEFENDI ANTÔNIO DA SILVA

live in a crowded stadium. There are memories of memorable games with you and friends, and more recently, you and I had become members again. But unfortunately, we only went to two games together, plus Ketynha. The last game brings back not-so-good memories because Ketynha got sick, and we had to go home at the end of the first half.

Maybe one day I'll go back there, my son, but it will never be the same. And it's no use people saying I have to go. No one feels for anyone because no one feels the pain that people feel. With all due respect, these are feelings from each person's private stories. Criciúma E.C. is still the only club in the world I root for, but now it's a secondary issue. My priority now is to work on my inner reformation, always aiming to improve myself as a human being, practicing charity in all its fullness and love for my neighbor.

I have learned that we are born into this world with the mission to love and always improve ourselves in goodness because love is the fullness of life. Only then, my beloved son, will I be prepared, by merit, to meet you again on the day my time comes to return to the Spiritual Homeland. I have chosen not to talk about personal matters here, as this is a memoir and not a biography.

So I decided to talk about my life as a hemophiliac and my grief. But I thank God very

95

much for the difficulties I have had and will still have as a hemophiliac because I consider it Divine mercy to teach me to live with difficulties and to redeem debts from past lives. Also, all the other difficulties I have had in the course of my life and others I will have, I consider blessings from God to teach me and to polish my spirit, which is highly indebted and in need of spiritual progress. The time is coming to finish this work, so I left it until the end to talk about your mother, my beloved son. The two of us had and still have the blessing of having her company. I usually say that whoever can't live with Zilma has some "problem." But someone might say, "Is Zilma perfect?" Of course not. If she were perfect, she wouldn't be here on Earth, which is a planet of trials and atonement. But I can assure you that she is a much more evolved spirit than I am and many others I know.

My son, your mother suffers deeply, and I do too. I try to talk to her every day and give her strength, because we know a mother's pain is different. If it were possible, I would suffer for both of us, because she is a good person and I hate to see her in pain. She puts on a brave face and wears a smile like a mask just to be able to work and face each day. It seems that as time goes by, people don't even notice, but we do, because time doesn't stop for anyone, and struggles and worries continue in everyone's lives.

DEFENDI ANTÔNIO DA SILVA

Life has changed radically, my son. Your physical presence is no longer part of our journey, and that's very difficult to deal with daily. There are days when the longing is so overwhelming that we think we won't be able to bear it. These moments can come at any time. When we are alone, we let the tears flow to ease the pain; when we are in company, we cry silently within our souls.

Oh, my son, your mother even tried, encouraged by me and true friends, to go back to the gym. She needs to keep active for her back problems, but she went for a few days and couldn't continue.

And how could she, my son? Since you were little, you both woke up at six in the morning to go to the gym together, sometimes by bus, sometimes catching a ride, and later by car, with you already graduated and being her personal trainer. How can a mother overcome such a tragedy? And sometimes she still has to endure comments from insensitive people. Only time, a lot of time, and a lot of faith and trust in God and in eternal life, can we manage to go on living. The weekends will never be the same, the nights... Oh, the nights, my son, have become somber and long. It is then that I perceive and see what no one else sees, nor could they, for these are moments of privacy.

97

A HEMOPHILIAC'S MEMOIRS: A TRUE STORY

Your mother's sleep has become restless, filled with sighs. Sometimes she wakes up crying, and when she is in a deep sleep, she has the countenance of someone who is crying. The truth is that a father suffers too, and greatly, as I do, but a mother suffers much more, that is indisputable.

You know, my son, unfortunately, I've heard comments that we don't feel much, that we got over it quickly, but we are at peace with this type of person who speaks without knowing and doesn't respect the feelings of others. In fact, they are people still attached to old dogmas and precepts who think that mourning means wearing black, playing the victim, showing a sad face and crying and crying. Acting like that has never been and never will be mourning, but rather the failure of faith and trust in God.

Neither the Bible nor any other religious literature asks us to do that. We suffer a lot, especially the longing for your physical absence, which is agonizing, daily, and forever. We are a family that loves each other very much, thanks to God and Jesus, but we have a lot of faith in life, which is eternal and never ends. Those who die lose their bodies, but not the light of life; the spirit continues to live on the other side. But who told you that? Our Lord Jesus Christ. Have you never read the Bible? Never studied spirituality in the various existing literature? Don't you believe? So that's it, we suffer a lot, but we are not worried about malicious comments. We are concerned with living our lives with dignity, doing charity, and never, ever rebelling against God, and never behaving rebelliously towards people.

The days have become sad and seem joyless. We miss our son very much, but at the same time, we know that we are not alone, nor are we the only ones in this pain and longing. Every day, every hour, every minute, someone delivers a loved one to the spiritual homeland. So, yes, we suffer, but many other brothers and sisters of ours also suffer every day. That's why we must be careful not to act selfishly and think that we are the only ones.

These are losses, longings, and stories that are different and unique to each person, but the feeling and longing for the physical absence are the same. Life has taught me that no matter how much we suffer, the clock of time does not turn back. So, suffering or not, our mission is to raise our heads and move on, even with our hearts in pieces, to understand and believe that we are travelers and interns in this time, in this place. We are here to redeem debts we contracted in past incarnations, and we are atoning for them in this one. However, God gave us the blessing of forgetting so that our triumph would be on merit, that is, through hard work in charity in every sense.

99

We will always have afflictions, as well as good days and bad days, but we will only emerge victorious from this life with a lot of faith and trust in God. I will end this work first with the prayer of Saint Augustine, then with a thought (reflection) from my first book published in 2020, which in my opinion is the "apple of my eye" of all my thoughts (reflections). It follows:

DEATH IS NOTHING AT ALL

Death is nothing at all.

It does not count.

I have only slipped away into the next room.

Nothing has happened.

Everything remains exactly as it was.

I am I, and you are you,

and the old life that we lived so fondly together is untouched, unchanged.

Whatever we were to each other, that we are still.

Call me by the old familiar name.

Speak of me in the easy way which you always used.

100

DEFENDI ANTÔNIO DA SILVA

Put no difference into your tone.

Wear no forced air of solemnity or sorrow.

Laugh as we always laughed at the little jokes
that we enjoyed together.

Play, smile, think of me, pray for me.

Let my name be ever the household word that
it always was.

Let it be spoken without an effort, without the
ghost of a shadow upon it.

Life means all that it ever meant.

It is the same as it ever was.

There is absolute and unbroken continuity.

What is this death but a negligible accident?

Why should I be out of mind because I am out
of sight?

I am but waiting for you, for an interval,

somewhere very near,

just round the corner.

All is well.

Nothing is hurt; nothing is lost.

101

One brief moment and all will be as it was before.

How we shall laugh at the trouble of parting when we meet again!

(Saint Augustine)

LIFE HAS TAUGHT ME THAT: The aggressor always suffers the most. Taking the first step towards reconciliation is not a weakness, but a virtue. One convinces with arguments, not by shouting. Serenity is a gift of the wise. Only good is the path to peace. Offending and humiliating someone will never prove us right. Happiness does not depend on financial condition, since there are people who live in mansions and are unhappy, and people who live in shacks and are happy. To be superior is to be elegant, distinguished, and noble, not arrogant, overbearing, and cowardly. Faith without works of kindness is dead, and we must love and respect one another, as Jesus Christ taught us. (Defendi)

And so ends this simple book of memories. Many things have been left unsaid, others have been forgotten, still others were not appropriate for being too "personal". Others, I did not write because I did not want to, because I thought they would only feed the so-called "gossipmongers" who do not even read.

DEFENDI ANTÔNIO DA SILVA

"After reading, I would be honored to hear your thoughts on this book. Your feedback, both positive and negative, is invaluable to me as a writer. Feel free to contact me via WhatsApp at +55 48 99620-2979."

"For those seeking support, "Amor que não se mede" (Love that Cannot be Measured), a WhatsApp group based in Brasília-DF, offers solace and connection to grieving families, particularly mothers who have lost children. If you are interested in joining this compassionate community, please reach out, and I will gladly connect you with a group administrator."

I would also like to mention that after the passing of our beloved son Jackson, Zilma and I created the "ACOLHIMENTO GROUP" (WELCOMING GROUP). We are already a group of 43 people united in charity work. Every month, we use the money we raise (donate what you can) to put together food baskets and donate them to families in need. It was the way we found (in addition to our faith) to ease our pain and longing, while also helping to heal the pain of others through charity. If anyone would like to join this chain of goodness and help us help, please contact us. Charity towards others helps me, helps those in need, and helps those we love who are now on the other side of life.

ADDENDUM: I mentioned that I was awaiting knee replacement surgery. Well, I had the surgery on 11/10/2023 and everything went well. I am very happy. I thank the entire Hemosc team - Cepon and the Hemophiliacs Association. Gratitude.

104

www.ingramcontent.com/pod-product-compliance
Lightning Source LLC
LaVergne TN
LVHW020911200726
843506LV00011B/1662